Labi Siffre

monument

First published in 1997
by Xavier Books
P.O. Box 17 Abergavenny Gwent NP8 1XA

Book Design by Keith James Design Associates
39 Charles Street
Cardiff CF1 4EB.

Printed in Great Britain by Mid Wales Litho.

ISBN 0-9520942-2-3

By the same author
from Xavier Books

Poetry:

NIGGER

BLOOD ON THE PAGE

A one Act Play:

DEATHWRITE

Representation: Eric Hands: 00-44-(0)181-677-9331

WebSite: http://dspace.dial.pipex.com/town/estate/ni67/

E-mail, Product & Mailing List: xav@dial.pipex.com

For PJCL as always

Monument

(For David Morgan "Mogg" Williams)

For the sake of their children they killed some of ours
in the battle for more   the circle game
is an endless game

When soldiers came to claim by right   the land
our fathers had won (in an earlier fight)
For the sake of *our* children *we* killed some of *theirs*
and the circle game is an endless game

But I do believe a new breed of heroes
will arrive sometime   refusing to fight
with anything less than the *only* solution:
that every child is *everyone's* child

Then the circle game will prove to be
a circle the brave will break

Stone Wall

He tells me that his father and two eldest brothers
make him kneel in front of them   his face upturned
as they unzip and piss into his opened mouth

to teach him how to be a man   aged twelve
red blooded   no more sissy
see the wrong of a girlish walk too easy tears his lack
of fighting back at play-ground bullies chanting fists of
"Carl's a faggot, Carl's a poof,
Throw the faggot from the roof!"

His old man pleads
"I've tried to beat some sense into that boy!
I've shouted till I'm blue in the face! I've done my best!
Would *you* want a pervert for a son?!"

His brothers laugh when the fair haired one says
"We give 'im a bit of toilet training, that's all"
and Daddy stands his ground explaining
"It's for the little sod's own good, don't you see!?
To shake him up!
Those buggers do all kinds of filth!
They spread diseases that kill!
And all you can say is
'This won't make him fancy girls'

But you don't bloody tell me what will!"

Requiem

She tells me how on her seventh birthday
her father *did it* to her

"Daddy's special birthday gift" he'd said
and placed her hand between his legs pressing
"this is for you"

then spread her like a rug and thrusting
gave her love the way till now she'd
trusting thought   all good fathers do

The same as where were you and what
were you doing
when you heard of Lennon's, Kennedy's
or Luther King's death

It's funny how you never forget
the first time you had sex

Everlasting

I not remember Daddy give me sign of love encourage
You can do it   You'll be fine   Don't worry son, I'll help you
Nothing like that

He bring us toys but he not play the game with us
on hands and knees
or buried laughing in Blackpool sand

He never join us on the floor in front of the fire
nor round the garden Cowboys 'n Indians
Never let us tie the willing victim to the chair
now *I* can't escape   his touch

was mainly for the hit
like when he teach me minutes hours
he move the hands he ask me time I answer
wrong he hit   again
he move the hands he ask me time I answer
wrong

he teach me much this way
but I learn only one thing

The Answer

We lived in fear of your coming home
"The Old Man"
Three little words that meant so much
remember

when I wrote the perfect poem
death
on my toy town tilting black-board   one word
that said it all though now in these uplifting times
the word would have to be *love*
regardless of the details

That you believed in Juju was a magic I had yet to learn
but in your shadow I could tell you were scared
"Did *you* write this!?"
and burning to hurt you more but mindful of your fists
my hate found fear
slicing my tongue to an angry silence

Remember when I knocked you down   me screaming
"leave her alone!"
three little words that meant so much I thought
till later when she made me say "I'm sorry"
by her bruises once again betrayed

As now weighed down with years more
than yours then   I'm cursed with second sight
and still you hurt me from the grave   of course
the answer is
If only you had hugged me once I could've been alright
I would've made that one hug last
my whole life

Six of the Best

It didn't make a better boy or man
of me
It didn't teach me right
Just taught me how to hate

It didn't introduce a novel point
of view
There being lots of hate already in situ

Sons of sons of sons of sons, I
merely joined the queue
of all those burning
to *do it* back
to you

Up and Away

The tree is wide awake ears pricked for the slightest sound
from the sun singing on the other side of all that navel fluff
If you hold a cloud to your nose I wonder what it smells of

Always when we've forced our way through the grey lake
with a definite plan for once knowing where we're going
I want to step out and bounce

from hill to hill I wouldn't fall to an insect death a splash
of red on the earth's bonnet   and I could too make my way
over the hills and far away if I could really mean what I feel

"Tell me a joke" I say "the one about the nigger
with a monkey on his shoulder"   "Where'dya get that?"
the white man says "Africa" says the monkey

"there's fuckin' millions of 'em over there!"
On the sofa I smile though the nigger is me
Do white folks think we hear the same joke
and won't they be pleased to know
I see a funny side

If God is white
Why should I pray
If I look up
He'll turn away

[I heard the last four lines in New York, attributed to an un-named, black schoolboy, aged ten. I hope he will allow my use of his work, which towers over mine, and accept my admiration of his talent. His verse deserves every available poetry prize, though I doubt the system's ability to recognize the depth, accuracy and power of his words.]

Home

(Every week in the UK, four children die from parental neglect or abuse)

I am of Great Britain   a provincial land
where Dunblane happens every four weeks
but nobody notices (enough to shout)
swear on TV and the letters *pour* out:
I keep a loaded gun in my head

I am of Great Britain   where love is something
you don't admit to   talent an attribute best
kept hidden (for fear of embarrassing the rest)
passion a weakness that threatens us all
and will never replace the Saturday night
beer glass thrust in the face:
I kiss you whenever I can

I am of Great Britain   where we teach our kids
it's OK to do evil if it means *real jobs*, besides,
if we don't... someone else will...

the official excuse for selling bullets to boys
who need bread and a bedtime story
mines and rockets to Rape, Pillage
and Swiss Bank Account Incorporated
and five hundred volt cattle prods
to regimes whose colonic, prostate, testicular
and gynaecological research teams
really have their citizens by the balls

sorry...genitals (I'd hate to give offence)
and I'm sure the whole house is with me
in offering support and sympathy
to *those* victims and *their* families

I am of Great Britain   a provincial land
where Dunblane happens every four weeks
but nobody notices (enough to shout)
swear on TV and the letters *pour* out:
and the gun in my head keeps firing
If, for even one moment, it stops, you have
my permission
to shoot me
dead

After a letter to the press from
Dr. Felicity de Zulueta. MSc MA (Cantab) MBChB MRCPsych
Honorary Consultant psychiatrist in psycho-therapy and clinical lecturer in traumatic studies.

Movie Movie

The handsomely man in the suitable suit
stands up in a fit as a very fit feline flow
leans over the restaurant table and punches her
_ bam! _ in the face
she goes down
hard

as a carving fork thrust to the eye   he walks
tall in the mightily   half the way round
the abandoned meal and kicks her three times
in the soft of her side   she cries out   no words
just an animal sound   a human sound

and the handsomely man in the suitable suit
pirouettes like a tank and targets the room
of knife wielding viewers   though some of us
only have spoons   as we sit transfixed
by nature well dressed in tooth and claw

he looks down   selects below the ribs
above the hips she gets the point
where the kidney lives
as he kicks her again and none of us move
and again with contempt he defies the room
dismisses us   turns and walks out

no one complains that their evening's been ruined
the waiters hurry nevertheless to assess
the mess the ambulance takes
twenty minutes to arrive

Primordial

he stands in the dark

rubs one credit card against

another   no spark

Long Live The Revolution

At this time of day the church doors are locked
If it's sanctuary you want
you'll have to make an appointment

In the mean-time would you mind
waiting over there in the usual ambience
of non-invasive music and magazines

Excuse me? Society moves at the speed
of the slowest? Well...maybe you're right...
but here at the service / client interface
we try not to mix philosophy with life

Besides, in reception there's all you could need
Cup of tea?
If you'll take my advice you'll postpone the ordeal
of an interview indefinitely

Wait till they've run out of time   pop your head
round the edge of the oak panelled door and wave
"Same time tomorrow?"
"Good sort, that"
they'll say

Premature Red Alert

"*I* used to be king!"
wailed the Angry-White-Hetero-Male

"There, there", soothed the Gay-Black-
Disabled-Fat-Woman, "It's only PR
nothing fundamental has changed

Though I no longer bow
when you enter the room, fear not
you still make the rules

And comfort yourself with this while I
determined, write a new page:

'We can change the world!'
cried the radical mouse
from the bench
by the statue
in the laboratory maze"

Open Day on the Estate

The lawns are lovely   pink and well kept   sweeping down
from the big slice of chocolate   cake to the kidney shaped lake
impressive though and two teas half grown with algae
and a couple of welsh-cakes please

It looks like the big house before the gruesome deaths pile up
on the plate   and the famous detective arrives to sort things out
a bit of a handful without any servants   watching
as two middle-aged men steal a kiss in the herb garden

These days the movie is too much controlling
There's a guided talk at half past three   a common mistake but
the bloke in the hat says it's Allium Triquestra   though it looks
and smells just like wild garlic

The cattle in the wood lie well away from the child
who won't stop the azaleas and rhododendron hills crying
he was only forty six

Yes, it's beautiful now, but it rained earlier
The calm before the hand of man is nature safely kept at bay
You can imagine how his wife must be feeling   by the waterfall
tumbling red and white and pink is everywhere till you said
"There's no hope really, when it reaches the lymph glands"

Courtesy Kills

When he visits   sometimes staying over and uses
the toilet to micturate   he always
lowers the seat and lid before leaving
the room   good manners   considerate after all
it's her domain and he assumes
she sits to pee

And when she's done with her twaa-let
she does the same for him but in reverse
and lifts the seat   politeness sake
for the guest and son who wants her not
to be his mother but his friend
a trick she'll never learn

And so from different continents they share
this conversation scribed in ritual
mirror messages of deferment
in the smallest room   he wonders

whether she is angry as he
denied
the selfish pleasure of giving
without return

Small Victories

Behind soft arm-chairs hunched in corners
clutching their knees to their chests under tables
backwards and forwards the backwards and forwards
rocking people cower

chewing their fingers flesh till the frozen
twigs beneath show ready to snap
they must have to can't stop
quivering like dogs on fireworks night

Surrounded by nerves thick with calluses her own
refuse to grow Sophie drops her purse coins spill
her shame she fumbles to her knees in a heat-wave
of blame as the checkout girl's face says "stupid cow!"
and the next-in-line-man stands too close his anger
threatening deserved blows

Was it true she was made in the image of God
No wonder he made such a mess: fighting, tears
and panic her breath a rasping curse in church she raises
ugly stains with a hand to the counter "I'm sorry"
she says, hating herself for meaning it

and takes the bag from the boy who filled
the tins of beans in first the eggs on top the body bread
the chocolate blanket walls the tampons of course a beacon
preside at this trial his smile knows all her bloody crimes

as she staggers through music designed to relax the fiscal fist
on and out to the street where she struggles to grasp
air
that grudgingly
allows her
to live

Smile You Bastard

Again the prospect of an empty bed

A couple o' more beers and then
It's a nice face   but not his face   so I think I'd better not

Lately walking out has seemed appropriate   though
I would like to know what happens tomorrow
So maybe I'll wait a few days
for more of the same I guess, you see

Marvin was wrong

There are few sensitive people in the world   and most
have little or nothing to give   or is this just me
having a bad day day?

Hey! Come on! Be positive!
The world is filled with worthy souls
sensitive and giving as mine...yes
that's what I was afraid of:

Your honour, I rest my case
After you in the hot bath
With the hemlock and razor blade

The New Neighbour

I am a camera he said

Shame about the lens cap I thought
but said

Don't get internal on me
let it out
let it all hang out

Adjusting the aperture of his flies he obliged
by soaking my sofa
with a steady stream of gold

The furniture and I were impressed
this man was after all in touch with his feelings
Bravo I thought and punched him to the floor

Liberation is a wonderful thing
till an anarchist moves in next door

A Night on the Rack

Another sauna in another town
I'd had my share   twice   and decanted
to the lounge for beer and cigarettes

Mid twenties blond six foot with blue eyes
a washboard stomach and all   he walked by
three times in three minutes   decided and settled
beside me his towel divided   well hung

I've been watching you was his opening line
you're handsome very but you know that of course
how old are you

Smiling I   how old do you think he considered
and chose thirty seven as flattering
enough to be safe without being absurd

Deep voiced he spoke with a saw toothed edge
you should workout he stroked his moulded chest
and give up cigarettes they're bad for your health

You're right I said but I'm set in my ways
he smoothed strong fingers along my thigh   I work out
for two hours five or six days a week   his fingers squeezed
it's a cliché I know but I really believe my body is a temple

I smiled   not for him   I was thinking of you
sixty nine with grey hair sturdy limbs and big belly
how you looked like an owl the night we met

And I rose to my rough soled cracked fifty year feet
nice talking with you I lied content
that *my* temple is in *your* body

After Prinsengracht

(Voor H.B)

3am   easing   backwards to my gratitude
your bearded chin resting on my   for you
strong left arm

outstretched   my right around your chest
your furry butt pressed warm against
the soft of me   rising

in you I sense the perfect night and mourning
for some childhood gift withheld
till now   you found that song in me of course

I read too much from your reply "I dare not think"
though time may show that you were hoping "found
at last"   as I am hoping now

Hello

Those who live an unfinished childhood
exist   bereaved   their eyes downcast

Their conversations   vague   distracted
though they learn to satisfy acquaintance
well enough

But those approaching with love in mind
or friendship   find the wall invisible
a micron thick   unbreachable   maybe
you could be the key

Come close and press your face against
the glaze to see the battle rage
the painfilled eyes the bloodied fists
and here   a muffled voice

In Case I Haven't Told You

You are my undivided attention
By far the universe's finest invention

An arms full of fun and comfort
The last of all things I'd want to hurt

Substantial   sturdy   solid state
Embroidered with whiskers you are

My autumn-winter-springtime-summer-
Elder statesman-Santa-beefcake

And when you lay your weight on me
You make me

Trapped   Free   Safe

"This time jew boy
I'm gonna break your fuckin' head wide open!"

the sky explodes
i dream i wake
confused and frightened
no mistake

the buffalo man with hippo wrists
elephant neck and silver-back's belly
can do what he threatens
to end my life
and still i want to fuck him

sometimes asleep i'm even more stupid
than when i'm awake
besides
i'm not jewish

The Foundling

on the edge of sight   just behind sometimes
the corner of an eye making fun of the notion
that I know *anything*

the sound of insect wings   in another room
in another house   in Afrika   no
that dream was long ago lost

"tender hearted" he said "you'll never change
your soul forever new born
naked, wet, arms outstretched   in the midst
of a battle that will not stop"

and then he kissed me   for comfort sake
misbelieving I was about to cry

and though he was not practised in this
believing

when he did
I did

Prague Under the Sheets

"It's half past tin", the other said, "the bottles are wilting"
This last was true as only the stubbornness of the table kept them
from melting through the laminate; the first however must have been
a misprint

A bird he was, waking to find itself frozen overnight to an unfamiliar
branch. Still, for love and friendship, and because they were yards apart
he tried to pour himself into the other   "It's ok" the other said
"I'm still half full"   death arrives and you don't notice

Overhead wheels turned four against four on an axis of crossed beams
which had no choice but to continue, betrayed so by sunlight

And as they turned the walls turned the room turned
the view through the windows turned the sky became the town
became the bathroom became the shore became the stairs winding
down to the great hall where the maid in her weary continued a day
three hours older and colder than his   and in which it was written

Drudgery is not borne with style
Emptying piss pots, collecting night soil, cannot be made to look good
on the catwalk or the video

But she had dreams of survival, leavened with a little comfort:
a corner to sleep, enough to eat, occasional words and few beatings
Modest dreams that raised her above his fears of appearing foolish
of being his own definition   though it was this fear
that made him worth loving

"Aren't you ready yet?" the other nagged. He gave no reply though
the sheets dishevelled over his feet shifted an uncomfortable secret
"If you don't get up soon, we'll be lit!"
and he wondered, "how long is he going to keep talking like that?"

Roots

Elements of this discussion herald my demise
though parts of me no longer living are discreet
as with music   not everything can be written down

Your home   your country   the country of the heart
home is where that is they say   and often affectation
till the solid waste assails the rapidly rotating cooling device

Then the country of the mind becomes the country of the soul
and you recall exactly where you left yourself
too late to struggle home

As when I thought you meant it when you said
I'm leaving   laid my continents to waste
important wetlands permanently drained

And so I am the brittle man
have mercy please
and don't do that again

Shallow Poem

I'd give it all up
for a lifetime
of sex
with you

I wouldn't get bored
or tired   I'd be happy
to screw and screw

and kiss
and suck and lick
and explore

then screw some more

You know
the crows
who testify
sex isn't everything

are those who don't get much
or anything

and boy
how they hate
to see us smiling

Small Bruises

I brought you my latest poem
You brought me a spelling error
"wrack" instead of "rack"
and then went back to the TV

documentary 'bout the Bossa Nova
surviving and thriving after thirty years
as we had   at that time

I wanted your attention   but that
was on the box   where voices sang
clear melodies fresh rhythms perfect
harmonies made of solitary   notes

The Devil I Know

Pegged professionally   tumbled by your expertise
I am an overdose of starch in the rinse   mocked
by the mobility of trees

Our love?
The annunciation made it immaculately clear
this birth would be still   but with God's usual
dislocution, the angel spoke only the language of cows
and we know where their pleas for clemency end

In vain my friends say this is a day for dancing
reminding me of the many public executions
like dinner last night at The Flying Fox
when you sneered over your crème brûlé
that you *could* have at *any*time

So why do I find me defending your manners
insisting pig headed to hair tearing comforters
that this gutting and slicing is a two way swing
You with your chainsaw
Me bleeding

Paradise Lost

Now that sex is dicing with death
many of us grow old before our time
withering on the trivial signs mis-diagnosed
a touch of flu   night sweats   wake up in terror
ease in the bath till the kick in the gut
from an unfamiliar blemish

For release from this he wanders through
the good old days
the high communion of anonymous sex
one to one   often many more   a pact
of hungry shadows   busy men
affirming their existence in the dark
to fight the light of "kill a queer for Jesus"
and the rest

His heart and flesh still soft   his soul
is woven now with steel and stone
A living monument to the maths of chance
this veteran of better times survived knows
too well   that even with a condom on
the good old days are gone

The Next Day They Saw Dolphins

conversation waned
we stood looking down
from opposite sides
of the broken seabird
black wings spread
clutching the shore
going nowhere to go
but slick enough
to light our way
lacking the spark
we wondered at this
creature
sideways head bowed
in resignation
the bird had sung badly
stolen eggs
killed
innocent chicks
we'd seen it all
the documentary evidence
but in self-defence
the bird would say
"I killed to live"

We killed our love for selfishness
for brief applause
(no, not for pride)
was for stupidity it died

The Price of Heroism

We sit divided by bread
disturbing this sign of friendship
on the kitchen table

Our dog under stairs on that rug you wove
lies curled
its ears pressed tight against its head

I lack that sense
of keeping out of things and lay my palm
on the back of yours

close
to revulsion you pull away   leaving
the stain of your hand seeping into mine

The Prodigal's Nose

When she knocked him flat
on his back the audience was shocked
by the amount of snot hay-fever can produce

He used that as an excuse of course
he'd have given as good as he got
had he not been so poorly

dressed in his striped rugby shirt
and corduroy bags he looked
like a bumble bee tipped out
of the dog's drinking bowl

Sodden, it took him a while to right
himself and by the time he was ready to fight
back she'd swung through the swing doors and out
of The Rover's Unwelcome Return

Treherbert Oct '96

Hard Ball

"Get over it"   you say as if
to a self-indulgent child   and she
knows how   to get over it

no tears
just-*ice*, another slogan,
fits her fist finger curling
the trigger she holds
the barrel to the hairs
in the hole above
your left ear lobe
and slowly
s q u e e e e e z e s

do you still
want her
to get over it

A Gathering Of Rainbows

(for Pride Scotland '97)

Is this the promised land
An island in the usual stormy sea
of wilful ignorance and lies

No matter rain or shine
Today I'm smiling...
Inside.

Out:
An exile safe in a family
of exiles by birth
destined for the front line

See, our numbers span the barriers
of gender, colour, creed,
abil' or *dis*-ability

This gathering of rainbows is in truth.
A nation strong. Enough to be
at home with itself and happily
with me

After Pitxot

(Antonio Pitxot: A Catalan painter)

There are stone people here
sense less
un yielding
feeling nothing

naked I bled
from their sharp
edges

till the day bells rang
in my queer black
hallelujah I

discovered how light
they are
easy to lift
up
throw
down

how easily
they shatter

For The Unknown Soldier

If you happen to be a Gay man try to be willowy, swish, a hint of a lady
the hands, a certain sway when you walk, nothing extreme, perhaps
a lisp, it reassures *them,* the hetero-folk, they like to be able to see
that you're Gay (as *they* define it) they like to think they can *tell*

If you happen to be a Gay man, remember to talk about beautiful boys
even if boys of any description are not your thing, and whatever you do
never say you screw men

'cause hetero males consider themselves *alone and exclusively* men
and nervous it makes them as hell to be told
that you've fucked in *their* group, to be told that some of them *like*
being fucked yes, nervous it makes them it certainly does
the poor dears

If you happen to be a hetero man what the tabloids call
a red blooded man
in a red blooded prison it isn't a crime to get sucked off by or to fuck
a man as long as it's only for sexual release on account
of there being no pussy in view

True it's more cred if you use the threat of violence to woo
an unwilling partner and best if a gang of brave arm punching heroes
corner a guy in the showers grab hold down spread
and gang-rape the cocksucker

Clinical cynical just to relieve the pressure's allowed understood
expected but if two men screw 'cause they care for each other
the sex tainted by, God forbid, love
then they're nancy boys, arse bandits, filth-faggots-scum

funny thing... you don't have to be straight
to be brain-dead, shit-scared, eyes nailed shut to the bone
but from where I stand, in no-man's land
it certainly seems to help

The Radical Poet Flunks

The drag queen MC had had eee-*Nuff*
of the drunk at the front and the rowdy
audience   she screamed
"If you don't shut up
I'll get a lesbian to sit on your face!"

and I thought
Thanks
for proving
you don't have to be straight
to be a bigot

And I watched
the rest of the show (neither bad
nor good)
but I didn't shout
out   in that crowded Gay man's bar
and I should

A Rose By Any Other Name

Fat men don't find love...apparently
Fat women eat instead...currantly
It seems the double chinned don't win
or wed   or get to bed the heroine
or hero

Scrupulously merry scoffing munching lunching
dribbling sauce on their soft
extensions   touch alone confirming
their genital pretensions

Content they survive making humans laugh
cheerful jolly green in the bath
so light on their feet   some of our very best friends
are morphically un-sleek

though only the beaux with aquiline poses
would get to water our daughter's roses
Streuth! We wouldn't want no great big belly
bouncing up and down on our Nelly

or hovering over her upturned fish
face
or reading the manicured news on telly
no close-ups if you please they tend to be smelly
and have to pay for it

Off Piste

In
love
both
sides
must lose
for both to
win the chasing
after images makes
poetry a thinly disguised
technique : avoid the standard
texts, beware the tired suggestions
of the great and good, who never wrote
a line of passion, snorted a few behind their
glass towers but never bared their genitals in
church : pay even less attention to their rules
designed to make a narrow education the well licked
path to being known as wise : for all our sakes be bold
rise up and do it in the street, frighten the horses to rearing
and kicking and rolling their eyes : though you suffer their lashing
hooves their vengeful teeth, before too long, though the pain will last
too long, their distant intellect will note you do them no harm, and soon
enough, though none too soon, they will return to peaceful grazing as you   move on

Up To Here!

The thing is   he said   his head in a cloud of red steam
As far as sexuality goes   heterosexuals have *never* had any balls

I mean more women are murdered each year in this country
by heterosexual men
than people are killed each year in this country
by terrorists

We're fighting a war against terrorists I said seeding the fertile ground
exactly he said his head taking root   perhaps we should be pursuing
a war against heterosexual men   women in the audience
nodded surreptitiously   I mean

it's unheard of for hordes of raging homosexuals
to sweep across continents burning bombing raping pillaging
slaughtering children and women machette-ing babies in half nailing
toddlers to mosque and church doors castrating
enemy soldiers stuffing
the victims mouths with their scrotums and peni and bollock
by bollock
before burning the bastards screaming alive at the stake

but for straights that kind of thing is traditional
they've always done it seems they always will
for straights that kind of thing is *natural*

yes I said but be fair
hets do suffer from a genetic aversion to mirrors

Dib Dib

When I was twelve my father wouldn't let me join the scouts
He thought they'd make me homosexual
his concern was eight years late   aged four
I had already recognised my self

though not by name the names were given later by the hate
filled ones who curse the voice and language
I was born with

So daddy warned severely (this was all the sex ed
he pronounced) that there'd be men who'd want
to put my "Penis" in their mouths

This didn't seem to me to be as nasty as it did to him
but I kept quiet not knowing why
someone would want to do this silly thing

Then less than twelve months later homeward bound
from viscous schooling I was found at Gunnersbury station
by a kindly waiter who served me well
and warmly showed where I fit in

I'm glad I didn't join the scouts
my father may have been mistaken
and I   might never have found out

a basis for understanding the simplicity of the universe

he the the the the the the the the the the the the the the the the
n sun sun sun sun sun sun sun sun sun sun sun sun sun sun sun
ed fed fed fed fed fed fed fed fed fed fed fed fed fed fed fed fed f
he the the the the the the the the the the the the the the the the
barley barley barley barley barley barley barley barley barley ba
ed fed fed fed fed fed fed fed fed fed fed fed fed fed fed fed fed f
he the the the the the the the the the the the the the the the the
soft soft soft soft soft soft soft soft soft soft soft soft soft soft sof
roated throated throated throated throated throated throated th
geon pigeon pigeon pigeon pigeon pigeon pigeon pigeon pigeon
ied died died died died died died died died died died died died di
s as as as as as as as as as as as as as as as as as as as as as a
uck buck buck buck buck buck buck buck buck buck buck buck b
hot shot shot shot shot shot shot shot shot shot shot shot shot s
ed tasted tasted tasted tasted tasted tasted tasted tasted tasted
flesh flesh flesh flesh flesh flesh flesh flesh flesh flesh flesh flesh
he the the the the the the the the the the the the the the the the
ked naked naked naked naked naked naked naked naked naked
lovers lovers lovers lovers lovers lovers lovers lovers lovers love
od stood stood stood stood stood stood stood stood stood stood
startled startled startled startled startled startled startled startle
he the the the the the the the the the the the the the the the the
farmer farmer farmer farmer farmer farmer farmer farmer farm
ursed cursed cursed cursed cursed cursed cursed cursed cursed
the the the the the the the the the the the the the the the the th
second second second second second second second second sec
rel barrel barrel barrel barrel barrel barrel barrel barrel barrel ba

After the Flood / Drought / Earthquake / Volcanic Eruption / Meteor Shower / ...

they kneel and give thanks
Oh Lord for deliverance
from the hell of this natural catastrophic disaster

alone in the crowd   perhaps not
but uneasy
with anger and guilt she can only wonder
from where did this natural disaster come

Analergy

The beauty of the world
you say
is proof   insisting
insistence wear the face of reason

I say

though I am transformed
with pleasure gasping
helpless bursting
in you with every
jet of semen
flooding upwards
knowing this is real

still

none of what I feel
is evidence
of your love

Considerations

(Notes for past and future poems)

The invention of the chapati is of far more importance
than the invention of gunpowder; and it is from this perspective
that we must re-assess our history and our place in the universe

◆

Absence of proof is not proof of absence
but neither is it proof, nor evidence, of existence

◆

The lie is not that God exists. The lie is that we know God exists.
After all, if you know God exists, then you don't have faith.
That's the whole point of faith… that you *don't* know.

◆

The third commandment says, "Honour Your Father and Mother".
Why is there no commandment to "Honour Your Children"?

◆

There are so many willing to kill and die for what they believe
So few for what they know

◆

Humans have a lazy and dangerous habit of promoting
"I don't know what it is… so it must be God".
Will we ever have courage enough to declare unembarrassed
and with no feeling of diminished self-worth
"I don't know what it is"?

◆

Society is the *direct* consequence of how we treat our children

◆

Jesus is reported as having said, "Give all you have to the poor and
follow me" not "Give a little of your millions to Christian charities
and I'll give you a knighthood".

◆

In order to adopt a child, prospective parents must first
satisfy a panel of authority, that they, the prospective parents,
are mentally, emotionally and financially stable,
and that theirs is a loving and committed relationship.
In order to have a child of your blood, all you need do
is find a fertile member of the opposite sex… and screw.
Why should children of your blood be so discriminated against?

◆

Religion is the human way of getting back at God

Dominion

It's a long way from jokes about farmers and wellies
and sheep   to this place
where they shock them to sleep
and take their breath away   for good

or bad
sheep don't miss what they've never had:
family albums, favourite songs, address books
and other essentials   but then
neither do human foetuses

Do sheep die
do they just pass on, pass over, pass through, pass away
do they   need euphemisms to deny
this traditional passion play

When they smell the blood of their fellows
do sheep pray

Don't Shoot The Piano Player Just Burn The Music

Consider:
Jesus Christ may well have been a schizophrenic
He displayed some classic symptoms of that chemical
imbalance in the brain that through the centuries
consigned such flesh to jail, the mad house, ECT
the rack and other tortures, sometimes burning
at the stake or canonisation   sometimes both

Consider:
What we're told by those who say they knew him well
That he heard voices and had visions and believed himself
to be the son of God   you talk to God, that's prayer
God talks to you, that's something less, society says
with one fork in its tongue

Consider:
That he drew our waking nightmare   terrifying views of
"Do unto others as you'd have them do to you"
No way!   That's mad terrain no sane and level headed folk
would venture   an unstable mind-field
littered with self-doubt   compassion   empathy

We have a duty, after all, and the right in law
to protect ourselves

I'll get the key
Good God in hell
Another one here for the padded cell

Pissing On The Dead

Invited to condemn
the latest bomb attack
from a "right to life" Christian group
protesting against abortion
homosexuals
and restrictions
on the sale of handguns

the TV preacher says
he supports anyone who acts
out of sincere motives

I
am eager
to meet him

Onward and Upward

And shall we desist from thistory
butcher birds on the needle tree

blood in our mouths
cool in the sun
these murders are fun

Oh Lord
Give us this day
their daily bread

and deliver us to be full

Amen

Porcelain

purity screams if you touch it deeply
polished white for the moment smooth
and waiting for grey mixed with oil
from the holes in my face

flakes of skin leave a message
of life after death after life metaphoric
as shrapnel exploding the jelly of a child's eye

we are spinning to time on the head of a rusted nail
leaning forward squinting to read the eternal messages
we miss the way home

snails on a mission of mercy beyond ourselves
seeing only ourselves   ourselves and our game
but with a prettier name

The Art of Life

"Don't worry it isn't as bad as it seems
You get used to it, most get to like it even"

With half his face, neck and left shoulder missing
and flesh shreds hung from the wreckage of bone
"touch it", he said, "you'll feel better"

I did, and I did   he was right it wasn't
nearly as bad as I had imagined
in fact I began to appreciate texture
evoking slick seaweed with small hard bumps

though not as grainy it making me smile
and the string with an artery pulsing it's length
gave a comforting rhythm a calming effect

"Is this the truth?" said the voice in my head
"Is this the truth?" echoed the soldier dead

"This truth is the greatest truth of all
 This truth will set you free"

The Systems

have always been in place

having nowhere to go

it is we who are cursed

with an ability to move

A Higher Coup

I must deliver

myself   God hasn't the time

and I lack patience

Chips

I

The white reviewer said he liked the black
writer's novel because though the black
writer's life had been blighted by racism
he the black
writer displayed
in his writing
no bitterness

Funny
how those
of the group
who do the kicking
so often want the kicked   to smile

II

Have you noticed how
when it's from Northern Nigeria
it's ethnic

but when Picasso does it
it's Art

III

Have you noticed how a poem
about a man and a woman romantically involved
is a love poem

but a poem about
two men or two women romantically involved
is a Gay poem

Adult Contemporary

I'm watching a singer I've never met
but to whom I'm distantly related
by business   entertaining
a group of D-Day vets
on the deck of a channel going liner

It's June it's sunny it's 1994
and it's time to commemorate the start
of the end of the second great war in Europe
time to reflect on the dead,   the casual dying
adrift in the water,   clutching the sand
soft on the streets beyond the beach

The singer's success in breaching the charts
is with heartfelt themes of love uplifting
nothing downbeat this troubadour gives
what the people want   listen
he's singing to old men in deck chairs
"there's nothing worth dying for..."

to men who will never forget the taste
of a comrades brains splashed in your face
or the feel of fear   warm in your pants
'cause the shell fell *that* close

and I wait and wait but it doesn't come
"isn't your child worth dying for"
or your partner   freedom from torture
or Zyclon B   isn't that perhaps
worth the risk
if the loss means so little
what's the value in having

but it doesn't come

Perhaps they weren't listening
or maybe the song has meaning less
than the seagulls tied to the boat with string
for these guys preferring Vera Lynn

or perhaps they suspect this limousine brain
thinks Adolf is Calvin Klein's new brand
of after shave
no
the bullet doesn't come

'cause maybe they know the space at the mic
with his song and guitar, is, and is singing
precisely, pathetically, fervently, worthlessly,
smooth, non-judgementally   nothing

Nursing The Dark

He disapproves when I write about blood
It's depressing   he says, and stops as though
It's depressing   is literary criticism

What else   I encourage   humour he says and irony that's
the way to get your message across
People are more responsive to humour and irony

But the poem's about the rape
torture
mutilation
and murder
of an eleven year old girl

I can't stop myself adding there isn't much room in that
for jokes

I suspect a whining note in my voice but he doesn't
seem to see my defeat and says
People want to be entertained...to be happy...to forget
the bad things

He's hammered the nail   and driving home
I determine to find a way to forget
B I TC H
carved deep in her chest
by a man who has no idea of how to write
good poetry

An Audience Request

Poets please   spare us comfortable poems
(usually with Disney-type nature near)
pleasant easy on the ear   nice poems to makes us feel
everything's all right   spare us poems approved because
they help us sleep at night

Bring us the world   rub our faces in it
show us the hurt   and our place in it
When we say we're not to blame, promenade before us
torturers, who, citing their duty to obey higher authority,
made the same claim
And if we'd say
we like that one about the crook-limbed, wheelchair pair
who fought the system   banished years of loneliness
with a tear jerking love affair
but was it necessary to display (where silky long and sexy legs
were meant to be) his twitching swollen head
between her flippered seal like feet   his dribbling tongue
between her dribbling lips   a frantic lapping at the door
till finding someone really wanted *her*   she begged for more
but with her palate split   her passion sounded more like "nnyawgh"

And if we'd intimate that in the one about the vicarage rape
we felt it was distasteful to have the villain thrust in time
to grunted lines of "Hail! Mary! Full of! Grace!"
If we'd mark such details out of place in poetry   for being
sordid, ugly, over the top
at least make us realise that long ago
we must have had our balls cut off
Simplicity
the farthest target   quiet, loud, you choose, but clear
not hidden soft in coy enigma cross-word puzzle veneer

In short   respect us
though we long ago exchanged self-respect for fear
Poets please   say what we're afraid to hear

Prometheus Again

And who has not sat in that chair
the one with leather straps
to accommodate wrists and ankles

the one with FREEDOM
embossed
on an offcut of tin plate

Who, tall enough to carve air
has not relaxed there   satisfied smiling
poised above the abyss

For a while and once I was so enthroned
till the spark I made from pain and struggle
ignited my soul   exploding the scales from my eyes
and tiger strong I sprang to self-knowledge

Oh yes   in this pleasant land
fools also
are permitted to write

The Death of a Poet

(for David Morgan "Mogg" Williams)

How can it be that you could make me cry
This is ridiculous   I hardly knew you

Two years eighteen months a year
No more   our meetings
less than half a dozen
yet today you made me cry

And I the sceptic who since the age
of reason found it hard to believe
good men or women do exist
am forced by you to reconsider this

and yes you made me cry

And I the poet who will insist
the courage to be vulnerable
is the most important part
distrust my tears   and rightly
as I do believe poets no more nor less
than priests or politicians
should be trusted less than the wind or rain

But I trust in you

Easier to do now that you're dead?
No, I trusted you from when first we met
at the reading of "A Distance of Roses"
your courage reinforcing my belief
one voice *can* make a difference

and yes you made me cry

and now you're gone
yet with me still
and I will not forget

(18th January '97)

Foreigner

"A refugee from the city?!" We rush
outside with ladder brush and bucket of paint
to change "The Crown" on the creaking sign
to "The Farmer's Laugh"   bitter
as the pint in his scarred hand

weathered outside as I am in
I won't be trouble won't be telling him
how he should be greener   twenty years on
his life is vital here and I'm just passing through

still losing the fight   insignificant   sure
but I'll never give in   never go back
though the voice inside says never say never
and fear shakes my beer hand spills
living liquid over dead skin

How's the shearing going?
I steady my glass with quivering lips
and drain life down in gulps   my eyes
on his answer   my mind far away
my head very nodding   my interest
will it be convincing enough
to fool us both

In The Ghetto

Out here we're on the edge
And don't forget we represent
The very best
And there are standards
And traditions to maintain

There is no need to wave the flag
In fact we all consider that
Bad form
But in the empire of the heart
We keep it flying just the same

Don't get me wrong
We like the Welsh
We love this land of song
But we brought our country with us
We don't need to belong

Incoming Calls

Thriving in the borders
we know we'll never be Welsh
but our children are   or will be
and we're happy to help

We're refugees from the cityscape
we came here to give them freedom
to grow
where the air won't line their lungs
with grey snow

Yes, some of us are ageing hippies
who art and craft and grow green vegetables
for seemingly little gain
but we add our incoming voices loud
to the chorus who want the village school to remain

We came here to join the community
though some fear we're taking over
'cause we want to protect what we came here for
when some who've been here for hundreds of years
want jobs no matter what the ecological discord

and some of your sons and daughters
can't live in the place they were born to
'cause some of us had loads of cash
from the sale of our city semi-detached

and we've forced the prices
beyond your dreams
and you don't see why *your* kids
have to leave

and it's happened before
It'll happen again
we can only try
to help our children be friends

'cause everyone wants a better life
and everyone fights to have it
and change is a river that flows on and on
no matter how much you damn it

Tongue Tied

She isn't Welsh
She doesn't *speak* Welsh
How can she *be* Welsh
She was born in Monmouth

Trouble is she *feels* Welsh
She wouldn't *be* anything else
and it hurts to be denied
by the zealot's jibes

They say the language
is all there is
She knows there's more
to being Welsh
than this

that the importance
is not the language you display
She knows the essence
is what her heart and soul
say

Across The Great Divide

The postman's wife and the colonel's lady
don't bother with who isn't Welsh and who is

They roll up their sleeves and muck in, they're brisk
There's a job to be done it's no use complaining

There's raffles and fêtes, first aid, cakes and teas
Hospital visits and meals on wheels

One votes Conservative the other's *Old* Labour
They're not afraid to dirty their hands
and they don't ask for favours

They know they're a cliché but those who laugh
don't visit Mrs Morgan who broke her hip
and needs help in the bath

The Heritage Trail

On

This

Journey

Never forget

To preserve your culture

You must

First

Kill

It